Wild Roses

Austin Poetry Society
Anthology 2025
75th Anniversary

Wild Roses

Editors • Thomas Smith
Benjamin Nash • Joyce Benvenuto

Transcendent Zero Press
Houston, Texas

Wild Roses

Each member of the Austin Poetry Society was invited to
submit up to 3 poems for inclusion in the anthology.

ISBN-13: 978-1-946460-70-7

Published by: Transcendent Zero Press, Houston, Texas,

Editors:
Thomas Smith • Benjamin Nash • Joyce Benvenuto
Design and layout: Thomas Smith and Dustin Pickering
Cover photo: Depositphotos, Inc Standard License
Author Dianazh414751412

AUSTIN POETRY SOCIETY

Welcome to the Austin Poetry Society. These are our poems. We have been a vibrant part of the Austin community for over 75 years. Our mission is to promote poetry. Our members write traditional and contemporary poems. We hope that you enjoy what you read in our anthology. Look us up when you come to town and together we will read, listen, write, talk, and learn about poetry.

Yours in poetry,

Joshua Kight, President
Susan Martinello, Vice President
Benjamin Nash, 2nd Vice President
Officers 2025-2026

Austin Poetry Society
P. O. Box 40981, Austin TX 78704-0017
Email: austinpoetrysociety@gmail.com
URL: www.austinpoetrysociety.org

The poets in this anthology write across styles and
subjects, but they share an impulse to connect—not just
through clarity alone, but through resonance. They address
the breadth of emotions: love, grief, joy, anger, fear,
loneliness, hope. Some of these poems unfold slowly, like
a conversation overheard in a dream. Others land sharp
and sudden, a flash of recognition. All are given as gifts.
All of them invite you to listen with more than just your
mind.

We thank you for sharing your poetry and yourselves.
Thanks to Josh Kight, Susan Martinello, and Benjamin
Nash for entrusting this venture to us. The poems have
brought us closer to all of you.

Austin poets, this is your Anthology. Be proud and enjoy.

Yours in poetry,
Thomas Smith
Benjamin Nash
Joyce Benvenuto
Co-Editors

AUSTIN POETRY SOCIETY

A History of The Austin Poetry Society
by Garrison Martt

The Austin Poetry Society was founded in March 1949 by
19 poets. Their purpose was to promote recognition of the
art of poetry, to kindle a finer and more intelligent
appreciation of poetry, and to encourage the writing and
reading of poetry. They elected UT Professor Dr. Robert A.
Law as President. In the fall of 1950, the group began
meeting nine months a year, following an academic
calendar of September through May.

Four members have been Poets Laureate of Texas over the
years: Aline Michealis, Jenny Lind Porter, Alan Birkelbach
and Karla K. Morton. Many Austin Poetry Society
members have been published and won awards. The Austin
Poetry Society began an Annual Awards Banquet in May
1959. In recent years the banquet ceased, however the
Annual Awards Program has continued.

The Austin Poetry Society often met in members' homes. In
1965 Poet Member Dr. Harry Groll Newton passed away
and bequeathed his estate (house, land and furnishings) to
past President Eloise Roach and the Austin Poetry Society.
It then became known as "The Poetry House" and became a
regular meeting place for the group.

Within 5 years the City of Austin exercised Eminent
Domain to purchase and destroy the property as the Mo-Pac
Highway was being built. Proceeds from the sale of the
house and its furnishings provided a $5000 Certificate of
Deposit for the Austin Poetry Society. Interest from this CD
is still being used for operating funds.

.

AUSTIN POETRY SOCIETY

However, membership with active volunteers slowly waned and by May 2020 the remaining officers resigned, with no elected successors. In addition, 2020 was the beginning the COVID19 pandemic and many social groups like the Austin Poetry Society were challenged to continue. With no leadership for the next season, the Austin Poetry Society would officially discontinue.

In response, a task group was organized in the summer of 2020 to re-imagine the Austin Poetry Society's By-Laws and reduce the requirements for the group to continue. The task group members included Garrison Martt, Bradley Strahan, Ben Nash, Kaye Abikhaled and Jane Fisher.

The task group decided to extend the 19-20 season to the end of 2020 so that elections could be held. Garrison Martt was elected President. Mike Jones agreed to continue as Treasurer on a voluntary basis. Jeffrey Taylor continued as the Newsletter Editor.

Members also voted to accept the task group's recommendations to update the By-Laws. The purpose of the Austin Poetry Society was restated "to study poetry, encourage the writing, reading and patronage of poetry, and celebrate the poetry of its members". Another change redefined the seasons on a calendar year basis (January through December) rather than an academic year basis (September through May).

Some of the other changes included:
Three elected officers instead of seven.
Twelve monthly meetings instead of nine.
Special contests instead of monthly contests.
Annual award programs now held in the fall.
No more standing committees.

AUSTIN POETRY SOCIETY

Membership paid on an annual calendar basis.

The old post office address was cancelled and a member's home address was used during the pandemic. The PayPal account was cancelled and payments were limited to checks and money orders. The non-profit status also lapsed.

In September 2020, the Austin Poetry Society began meeting virtually with Zoom. Derrick Hughes was the first Zoom presenter. The first annual calendar season began in January 2021 and Dillon McKinsey was the presenter. Virtual meetings allowed some members to live in other Texas towns and other states. The group was no longer limited by geography.

Mary Jane Philpy-Dollins was elected president in 2024; she also volunteered to serve as interim treasurer. The Austin Poetry Society began gathering occasionally at Austin locations (often hybrid meetings using Zoom) in addition to regular virtual meetings. A Venmo account was also established to allow electronic payments again.

Joshua Kight was elected president in 2025. The Austin Poetry Society continues to meet virtually using Zoom while also meeting in person occasionally. Membership has grown to over 40 active members. The group now has an official post office address again (P.O. Box 40981, Austin, TX 78704). In addition, another member anthology is planned to celebrate The Austin Poetry Society's 76th year.

July 2025

BIBLIOGRAPHY

Austin History Center – Austin Poetry Society Records
https://ahc.access.lyrasistechnology.org/repositories/2/reso
urces/1999.
Austin Poetry Society By-Laws, 2024.
Austin Poetry Society Golden Jubilee Anthology, 2000.
Austin Poetry Society Yearbook 2010-2011.
Austin Poetry Society Yearbook 2012-2013.
Texas Commission on the Arts – State Poets Laureate
https://www.arts.texas.gov/initiatives/texas-state-
artist/statepoets-laureate/.

Greg Silver passed away recently. This anthology is dedicated to him. He was a good friend of the Austin Poetry Society for many years. He loved poetry, books, and music. He enjoyed sharing his spirit, creativity, and his writing abilities with others.

AUSTIN POETRY SOCIETY

if then Truth

if then Truth is the asset we value the most
are we willing to lie to protect it?
if we're dealt losing hands might we deal off the bottom
so justice prevails
as corrected

children lie all the time - the adorable tykes!
garner smiles if they cutely deny it
but there may come a time when their parents discover
they've waited too long
to decry it

much the same undeniable verity holds
when society tolerates evil
even though what gets broken might be none of ours
no, the neighbors won't pay for it
we will

Magna

decision falls upon me
as I clear the shelf at last
in the form of a diploma
simply framed behind the glass
how revered, this vaunted parchment
its *Cum Laude* 'neath her name
even *Magna* added to avouch
how warranted her fame

but should I save or send to trash
this *Magna*'s humble splendor?
it serves no purpose I can find
nor can its loss offend her

so I shall place it in a drawer
and when I pass, the painful choice
will fall less heavily on him
who may decide by wit or whim
what is there left to learn, and why
now dust has sifted through the pores
the question passes then to him
the paradox endures as yours

AUSTIN POETRY SOCIETY

The Gift

If time is all we have, my love
Then dreading each new dawn
Was such a mortal waste of life
Its promise all but gone

To wake and wish the day were spent
Lest it bring only gloom
It was a living death of sorts
With life its waiting room

But now I find I vault to life
Each dawn as daylight breaks
For just the thought we'll meet again
Is all the spur it takes

And more, the priceless consequence
Of vanquishing my sorrow
You've guaranteed this simple gift:
You've given me tomorrow

"A Cliché of Months"

Janu—airy, you're a flurry of fresh air,
resolved— the umpteenth time—and never give a care.
Fi-bruary tells no lies. Don't lie, don't fib!
Hand me a heart-shaped chocolate nib.
March in like a lion, March out like a lamb,
you think spring is here, and a blizzard hits. Bam!

May I blossom or May I not?" depends on the weather, whether or not—
a heat wave? an ice storm? depends on what you've got!
Ju-next, dju last, dju always stay— ninety miles south of Floriday
Ju-ly to me again? Ju-lied to me before. Half the year is gone,
I want more and more.
Au-gust of wind will blow it all away:
shriveled leaves and ice cream cones, Fall is come to stay.

Swep-tember did I say? will sweep it round and round
ghosties and goblins, a maelstrom most profound!
Acht!-ober- yellow leaves, brown and foamy beer
Yah I'm so happy, Oktoberfest is here!
Nov-remember last year, when turkey was the king? Cranberry stuffing,
and grandma's pumpkin ring.
Here we are December, when Decent rules the world. Advent and angels,
Holy dark night. A star in the sky removes eternal blight.

"Time Enough"

A minute is enough time
for a hummingbird to drink its fill
before it makes its way across the sea.
To wonder, how can that be?

To plant twelve radish seeds,
one at a time in an egg carton.
Then take a bite, when they're red and ripe.
To pray for the peace of Jerusalem

A minute is plenty of time. Plenty.
to swoop down and pick a flower.
(It really doesn't take a whole hour.)
To make a wish

Bees don't take more than a minute
to sink into the sweet nectar
of a cornflower, a cherry blossom.
To breathe in. Deeply-four breaths - more

You say you're pressed for time?
What else do you have to do. What else?

"Don't Critique This"

I'll just go ahead and dip
my toe into this poem.
Or maybe, let's say—tread lightly.

I can snake a word around the
end of the line,
pop it onto the next one, and
tie it up in a bow.

Oh, I can let sleeping dogs lie—
it's a horse apiece if you know what I mean.
But I don't want to tell you about my horse.
I do mix metaphors.
Oh yes—they take me where I want to go.
My muse is in the driver's seat so
it's easy enough to saddle up and ride.

This poem can get the best of you—
it's maddeningly slow, quite frankly.
and not going anywhere soon.
And one more thing :
Leave your glue gun at home
Post-it notes will do.

You may want to reposition them
here and there, on my pauses and breaks.
Why would you, come to think of it?
but if you do
please fix up my poem, put it to bed
and slap a bow on it. There, that's that!

The Story of Cranes

They fly so high
above the clouds, below the sun,
so high you can't see them.
You can only hear them,
bubbling—like fountains,
waterfalls of sound.

And they land—here.
Thousands, so that you turn
your head to see them all.
They are here—for rest, for water
and maybe cheer each other on.

They have come from Mexico,
fly through the growing arc
of returning sun.
They are going to Manitoba
far beyond the winding Platte,
up and over the far Dakotas,
over one more Border line.

I have a pendant.
I wear it once a year.
It's a copied petroglyph
found on a rock from early time.
That means an artisan soul too,
a thousand years ago
heard sound in the vast blue sky,
saw birds descending from clouds,
and wondered like me...

Infinite horizon, what stories
you share and tell...

That Shooting Star
(in memory of Duncan Walker)

You drove too fast.
Your deep laugh could be heard
gliding the hall to fill other rooms.

You showered your love with affection,
heeded her sparking thought.

You were the son your parents dreamed
they would always have.

A friend to all--
homeboys who swung with you
high in trees from limb to limb
or climbed tall danger rocks, leaping
without falling.
From East to West you traveled
blazing across night sky.

I remember our campfire
you always built.
The lake quiet with a fish jump
once or twice to startle the night.
The boat tied with only the tic-tic
of lapping waves on the metal lift.
We told stories,
and then you would see the shooting star.
Your head would lift, your arm
outstretched
"Quick, Grandma, look. Don't miss it!"

But I do, that shooting star.

AUSTIN POETRY SOCIETY

Responsibility

I do not like to cook.
I do not—read cookbooks for fun.
I do not have conversations
about your food, my food and what spice.

But I cook.
It is my responsibility.
I get it done
because after all, we eat,
and someone has to feed us.

At the end of my dock
is a spider. I call her Florence.
She minds her web. She has babies.
I watch two of them.
Every day, she repairs
what the birds have torn,
and her little spiders grow.
She knows her responsibility.

Florence and I cannot control
the whirlwind in the trees,
nor the waves, striking the stones of the shore,
nor the morning rabbit who eats
all of the milkweed leaves.

We must settle for our small domains
that need attention
like Cheerios strewn across a table.
We are caught in our web of responsibilities
like them or not.

We get them done.

Rainforest

Brightly winged rainbows appear to swiftly float by,
 soaring, gliding, and hovering over the emerald trees.
The birds of the rainforest spread their colorful wings,
 hitching a ride on a scented evening breeze.
This paradise is where the gates are open for flight.
They say the Eden of Garden was hidden in a vast
 tropical rainforest.
Wild animals sniff the air as some leap into
 a crimson sunset.
A few monkeys swinging from one branch to another.
The rainforest is adorned in green by mother nature.
The forest floor is abundantly covered with plants
 used for medicine and healing.
Taking pictures and shooting videos of this beautiful
 paradise is very gratifying.
Nothing man creates compares to this natural beauty.
The thought of its destruction is saddening.
Hopefully one day mankind will stop
 destroying these beautiful rainforests.

AUSTIN POETRY SOCIETY

Sunrise Over the Mountains
The sun rises another day far beyond the mountains.
A lasting, lingering shadow washes away with its soft glowing light.
The sun stands tall over the valley of dry land while the creatures
　　of the night seek refuge and shelter from the heat.
As the sun begins its golden rise above from behind
　　and over the mountains, the fog disappears as the
　　mountain range comes into full view.
A gentle breeze blows in the early morning before the heat
　　becomes intense.
The land in the area has a purple haze that reveals an
　　uneven desert landscape.
A drifting hawk soars past in the early morning while it is
　　still cool in the desert valley.
Some of the land is eroded from the acid rain leaving a
　　layered look on the rocks.
Stillness lingers as non-living things appear dry.
The desert plains look lonely beneath the blue sky
　　as the living desert welcomes the new sunrise
　　and a new day.

Waterfall in the Garden

I listen to the gurgling and burbling sounds of the waterfall
as it cascades over a cliff and down into the valley,
making its own path.
While standing near, I can feel a cool mist on my face.
You can hear the echoing sounds while sitting, standing,
just walking by.
The flowing stream leaves a trail of pleasure as the
waves sparkle when the sun beams down from up high.
The mist keeps everything cool and refreshed.
The plants retain the moisture and their foliage remains green.
Waterfalls are often under appreciated.
They provide an unspeakable beauty, relaxation, and provide nourishment
for many plants and animals.

Cities

I'll meet you in New York City where the streets are bustling
and we try to get a word in
without being distracted by people watching.
We will smile at this serendipitous moment of how far
we've come to be here, coffee drinking, across the country.
We will go our separate ways though.
It's my torturous dream to sit at a coffee shop with you in New York City
thinking, naively, a change in scenery would save us.

You, in black and white will pop up like a facade on streets
with so many people, blurred.
I'll be disoriented, but would never tell you the truth.
I wish you had been enough for me.

The parks will be beautiful and the food will taste good
And I'll pick myself up off the grass hands to the sky
Strong legs and abdominals.
Mourning.

Did you know Balboa is bigger than Central Park?

I predict the city will lull me, it may not be my saving grace,
But God, something will
One day.
We are expected to grow, but not grieve. Grow, but not mourn.
Even a flower weeps her petals.

Laughing, giggles, people watching, happy faces.
I will continue to live out my dreams.
Continue to connect with the aroma of joy and embody aliveness.

Your shadow of a silhouette will creep up into my head
Fighting for space.
Sadly, I breathe into the unknown, alone,
maybe sitting on a floor in New York City,
meditating on candlelight bouncing off red Moroccan carpets,
or whichever city I discover myself (without you) in.

Neighborhood Ghosts

I had a huge meal tonight
a rowdy hibachi family feast
coming home and feeling stuffed
I stepped out to take a brief walk
in the crisp New England woods
needing to clear my overloaded soul
not to speak of my poor distended belly
I stumbled along under muscular clouds
interspersed with cold fierce stars
huge shadowed Oaks and Pines lined my path
hearing the distant clank of goose calls
I could see through the thin veil of time
travelers on this ancient road
Native brethren carrying children
or perhaps
a tired colonial farmer on the seat
of a wagon hurrying home
for his dinner

Black Bird

Today I saw
the end in me
way back there amongst
the breakfast crumbs
A black bird
stalked among the coffee cups
pulling the table cloth with
his nails
Quick and silent he stabbed
beak- nailing the scattered
moments and rattling the spoons
His blackbead eye cocked
speculative and
thinking of lunch

The aging mind

The river slows
and backs up behind
a massive concrete dam
banks rimmed by
sun washed granite boulders
bounded by the tangled roots
of overhanging spruce
deep in watery green depths
lie old snags and branches
carried by storms untold
mottled and dimly reflecting
the distant sunlight

High in the pitted wall
a small sluice way
releases a restricted foaming
violent stream of water
over the edge and into the
shallow and rocky outflow below

Against that unrelenting stream
Shiny muscular fish strive to swim
against that onslaught
only a few battered survivors
scales torn and colors muted
make it to lie in the quiet depths
wishing they were birds

a whirlwind tour
with my Eurail pass
dad's pending surgery

on the night train
alone to Lausanne
a strange man
bends to my face . . .
winter rain

empty arid earth
where the train station stood . . .
now my car
bumps over old train tracks
and memories

Retirement

after Ada Limon

bursting backwards the
fences, undressing a once dressed land
me and
my wild heart
I am, we are
raising down order
rewilding

Ode to Pencils

in an old chipped mug,
slender bodies of wood
pinched from faraway places,
my companions lean
heavy with memories

but light to the touch
unlike pen and ink so heavy and officious
pencils, so humble they take no offense
at being erased

these wooden marvels allow words
to roam across the page,
lightly like tumbleweeds on soft sand
idling away their time doodling

you can have a beer with a pencil
tucked behind your ear
wine requires a fancy pen
but a pencil is like an old friend
the words come easy

too relaxed for official documents
except #2 pencils on bubble tests –
for my purposes,
my delight
a pencil is just right

The Garden Apron

I planted my tomatoes and basil today
wearing the garden apron my mother gave me

the same one I rolled my eyes at
as I did with so many things from her

like the timer that you hang around your neck
so as not to forget what's on the stove

I haven't worn the apron much,
yet the fabric has a well worn feel

covered in plants of orange and green

a pocket just right for a smartphone

and tools easy to grab
but I rolled my eyes

I had no way of knowing
what a gift she was giving me

it's just like her to be
so indirect

preparing me for old age
in her circuitous way

and now there's no way
to tell her "thank you"

Prairie Dog Town

When I think of Texas Critters
I think of the Prairie Dog Town
Endless source of delight for children
The very first time I saw owls.

Burrowing Owls perch on the entrance to the tunnels
Small hawks circle, industrious little round furry
Prairie dogs stand on their hind legs barking
The ground alive with critters.

When I think of the ground alive I think of the
Complex of burrows and intricate tunnels with
Built-in drainage in case of flooding,
All hidden from view.

When I think of hidden from view
I remember romantic notions from childhood
Prairie dogs, owls, rattlesnakes, spiders
Black-Footed Ferrets all at home in the colony.

When I think of the colony today I know
Prairie dogs are the Chicken McNuggets of the system
Builders of refuge from sun and predators,
Many species depend on them
For housing, then eat them for lunch,
Many resident in their life-saving burrows.

The Prairie Dog is 90% of the Black-footed Ferret's diet.
Who are the Chicken McNuggets of the human colony?

The Horned Toad
Phrynosoma cornatum

Is there a critter more Texan? Looking remarkably like a
Very small *Triceratops* or a very large armored diatom
They stand their ground, spitting blood to the delight of small children.

As a child I discovered if I got down on the ground and was very still
The Horned Toad would stop spitting, cock its angular little head and
We could talk for hours in the language of children and critters.

This discovery lead me beneath the neighborhood church (not my own)
Built up on concrete blocks. Wanting to take my new friend home,
And after successfully coaxing her into a shoe box, I became stuck.

Crying out for help, a neighbor heard my cries and alerted my mother.
I don't remember how I was freed from this earnest enterprise.
I do remember my mother's patience.

The flies we collected to feed my friend, (who prefers to eat ants)
And the gentle coaxing that, after a time, we should set my friend free.
Phrynosoma cornatum – most Texas of critters. Little but mighty.

What were we thinking as we gazed into each other's eyes?

HOLD FAST
Conversation with The Thread – Wm. Stafford

There is a text:
"Feed the hungry, welcome the stranger
House the homeless, care for the sick"
This is my thread.
Will the thread keep me from the edge or
Will the thread led me to the edge?

When I was young I hoped
The Thread would lead me to the edge
Later in life I held on tight
Hoping the thread would keep me
from the edge.

I remind myself
"while I hold the thread
I can't get lost".
Even though it goes
Among things that change.

This thread goes missing
When I am not mindful.
I always find it
At the edge.

In times of loss and fear
In days of chaos and despair
"Hold fast to your thread" I tell myself
Never grow weary of where the thread takes you.
As long as you live hold fast to your thread.

The Arizona Baptism

Hours
and miles to divine amnesty, a sinner –
dehydrated and metal-scratched
by capitalism –
stutters through rehearsed words
for a private conference.
Sonoran waves on the horizon welcomes
a thirsty robot, as he leaves Texas
skyscrapers in the rearview mirror.

To be drenched in light
from the turquoise above, the dry soul runs
towards middle ground – his absolution
on a stretch of road between mountains.

Forgiveness seems conceivable
in Arizona – where the clatter of machines
could be soaked to silence.
Clanging resounds from the ladder, but an
ethereal tsunami waits for industrial drifters.
Suits trample each other still, and
God's voice roars to direct me into refuge.

"Rain on me and recover my heart"
an android imposter calls out
to the beyond.
Sunlit rays –
from *celeste* into *ultramar* –
will pierce through
any three-piece armor and necktie.

Optics Taught by Ms. Alice, 2008

Ms. Alice encouraged self-reflection
to face the rabbit hole –
adult life best lived in business uniform.
If one must wander through Topsy-Turviness…
a looking glass
could magnify keys through bolted doors, my mentor said,
and perhaps safeguard a political adventure.

No one could have corrected me in denim, my tunnel
vision
would lead towards marvelous destination.
Who knew, then, that eyeless arrogance
would belittle me to tears yet inspire growth?

In Wonderland,
my outspokenness could not outplay hierarchical arguments.
Into fun and games,
through vast wilderness,
I followed reappearing smiles until
a royal house of cards toppled my outsider curiosity.
Ms. Alice was right
I grew to learn,
the final – and only – word
wouldn't always be mine.

Reverent
to the grains of sand in corporate hourglass,
a taller reflection is now displayed
inside my cheval mirror –
tweed on both sides, the protégé grins
like a mischievous cat with a secret.
I'm ready for the Tea Party
and its inescapable punch-clock.

The Next Stage, 2022

In a bar patio,
the microphone waits for a ready flyer.
Wordsmiths – at pupa stage –
have gathered in El Paso from all over Texas.

The runway hums at us
like a lullaby to soothe acrophobia.
Winning words,
by their own creator,
should not be cocooned forever.
There's a chance for a rough takeoff at the mic
but
Chrysalis,
protected by pixie dust,
should dream of the best views.

I notice she trembles in line,
the Austinite
preparing herself for metamorphosis –
a private wish set to fly
as a universal truth.
She wants to soar but misses her abuela,
the north star lives now in memory.

I also want to fly,
and learn aerobatics for any crowd.
The right wind
to correct my glossophobia
could be found in the desert.
El Chuco –
away from *Dallitudes* and their skyscrapers –
seems like the right place for first-time magic.

AUSTIN POETRY SOCIETY

Modern Day Civilian's Basic Training

"OK, Everybody, take a knee!
Lift it off each neck you see
being pressed to death's grim door.
That is *not* what knees are for!

If Forced to Change Color

If forced to change color like these leaves of Autumn,
would I be the red, orange, yellow or brown?
Forced to let go when the chilling winds blow,
would I relish my low-lying view from the ground?

Would I be pressed in an old family Bible
rarely exposed to the light of the day,
or would I be raked up by eager young children --
then bagged up like yard waste that ended their play?

Would my new persona as a leaf that has fallen
add to the good herbal hint of decays?
Could *I* be the fodder for new leaves unfurling
into breeze-quaking, shade-making habits of praise?

Could There Be Such A New Creation?

Rumors of pending
annihilation
make some folks crave
a New Earth's Creation --
this one filled with
godlike wonders yet unknown.

Perhaps the *next* Earth's Generator
could make a planet even greater,
well-staffed by caring crews
on *every* side of its equator --
and preserved as if
it were a precious stone.

Lasting Peace could rain
on this New Earth,
making All Life On It
feel it's worth --
get to see at last
injustice overthrown!

Blessed by Limestone
With thanks to Barbara Kingsolver

No creek runs here in August.
Beneath this bridge, just fossil-laden stone.
Melted bones of April's minnows
merge with skulls of plesiosaurs.

I come at moonrise, listen to secret tides –
whispers from an ancient, teeming sea.
Instead of still-hot concrete, newborn sand.
Instead of city-light-washed sky,
a black, sparkled dome.

Stars that shone then still send light my way.
Rhythms of that vanished ocean
echo in my veins.
I walk home, knowing I belong
to sediment, to firmament,
to worlds extinct, to places yet unformed.

Class of 1965

Our year was 1965.
Elvis was still alive.
Graduation came and off we went.
Problems in Vietnam were evident.

Some would go to college for a class or two.
Others became busy with work to do.
Some would marry and become a wife.
Lots of adventures started in our new life.

For guys, there was a draft in effect.
Military service was expected without physical defect.
Some would go to college causing a delay.
But we all knew we would have our day.

Vietnam would take its gruesome toll:
Taking the life of men so young and bold.
Many would serve, expecting to die:
But return after serving, thankful to be alive.

Time moved on as we began to settle down.
Some ventured away from their hometown.
Some grew old; others were destined to die.
Life's not fair as we look back with a curious eye.

Now 60 years have flashed by,
Since graduating from our hometown high.
Eighty years of age is approaching soon.
Yes, we were part of the baby boom.

Twenty-two percent of our class have passed away—
So, be thankful for each, and every new day.
Now, it may be time to start a new career.
So, start a new adventure like Moses did in his 80th year.

Looking for Food

I went about looking for food.
Some say I am ugly and rude.
To eat I patiently wait.
It's part of my character state.
Now, this may sound strange.
Cars help provide food on the range.
Cars kill deer you often see.
I think they do it just for me.
As I fly over and carefully look down,
I can detect a dead one on the ground.
I am a buzzard always on the go.
Cars are my friend you now know.
I am part of God's cleanup crew.
Be thankful for the things I do.

Senior

As a senior, I arose kind of slow.
Nevertheless, later to class I would go.
I had been to this class many times before.
On this day I was scheduled for one more.
The wild and dynamic teacher we could not ignore.
She had her own unique way that we did adore.

I was a repeat student having taken the class last year.
I needed more instruction that was clear.
Learning new tasks and maintaining skills was the goal.
Thus, I went to class, participated, and as told.
In this class I strived to work on my core.
The teacher was kind and did not keep score.

This was a senior year for me.
I was a repeating senior you see.
As students, we encouraged one another.
Thus, we improved and advanced our skills further.
With the work we do, it seems sad to me:
That this class does not count for a degree.

How could I be a senior in this class for so long?
It is sort of like an age-old song:
With a repeating melody.
Understand, many of us are over seventy.
It's an exercise class where we have a ball.
We work to stand straight and avoid a fall.

Ode to unknown poet

Solstice Eve
the East Coast snow
caps autumns colorful display
ignores the South, still baking
praying for oven buzzer to ring.

English department at small college
just shy of the desert, releases their
yearly journal containing an offering
about dancing in the rain
phenomenal poem
reprint of a big name.

The President and Congress
strike a deal on perceived Armageddon
while sacrilege of a different color
bursts out of a Hollywood icon.

Both stories blaze nova hot
a five-minute epiphany
then bus doors close and WiFi cuts out.

Turkey has an earthquake
Taiwan a riot
and a mine in Brazil collapses
causing the world amethyst market
to be affected for twenty minutes.

Another section of planet
slides to the dark side
children and puppies are put to bed
parents breathe a sigh of relief
pack lunches because first period bell
will ring tomorrow at 8 a.m. sharp.

Wishing cannot make it so

Every afternoon my steps lead
to the cemetery, sunny or drear weather
does not decide me.

When budget allows
I leave flowers, trinkets,

I've burned
many a candle,
potion
or Gris Gris.

Yes, I cry silent desperate
tears, seasoned
with frustration.

I cry for the good times
that will not come,
the loving caresses
I will not have.

I want to feel comfort
in this desolate area
but my heart breaks
because he is still
not buried here.

There is a cottage on Killary Bay

      where blue-eyed man
entertains with passionate
deluge   fairy tales
and famine stories.

Late at night
he produces, badly bound
dog-eared book
reads the old poems
of this land's blood
and stone.

First, in their original tongue
to hear the rhyme's music
feel
the Irish melancholy.

Then translated
so I'll endure
the weight of loss.

The water is blue, but not blue.
It's green, or grey or burnt silver,
far beyond the scope
of anything as mundane as words.

History here
is a stew of fact and tale.
Just like the Selkies
with their blue eyes.

The Little Boy in Me

The little boy in me made me eat the apple pie on the sill.
The little boy in me made me splash and swim naked in
the rill. The little boy in me made me dig for worms in my
Sunday clothes and leave Dad's tools out in the rain. The
little boy in me made me play hooky from school to go
fishin' with the guys again. The little boy in me made me
build a fort to keep the wild Indians away. The little boy in
me made me become a chief worthy of a ransom the very
next day. The little boy in me made me sing those hymns
loud to keep the devil at bay. The little boy in me made me
pull the braided hair of the girl I liked in class in a very
tender way. The little boy in me made me write my name
so eloquently in the driven snow. The little boy in me
made me sail my pirate ship in the hearty winds that blow.
The little boy in me made an adventure of every day. The
little boy in me made me the man I am today.

The Carousel

The carousel spins 'round and whirls all the the little cowboys
and cowgirls. Spurring their steeds as they jump and prance,
leaving their riders in a two minute trance. Folks watch with
a gleam in their eye, remembering carousel rides from days
gone by. The music is gay and laughter abounds, as the riders
gallop happily on the merry-go-round. The carousel slows
from its fanciful flight, then riders dismount with luscious
delight. Another group awaits for the galloping spell to take
their turn on the carousel.

Aged Soul

Do I applaud that tinge of grey or do I cover it with black?
Is the wisdom that I've gained worth the time I lack? Do
my aged eyes see differently now from the days long past?
Every sense remembers how I arrived here so fast. I
thought I'd live forever and there would be no way that I
would turn so old this fast looking forward to each day. So,
cherish your youth while you can, it vanishes to fleet, and
keep those memories of the times when life was fresh and
sweet.

The Comedy of Being Us: We Are All One

We wake with plans, ambitions bold and bright,
But fate, the jester, trips us in our flight.
The coffee spills, the day slips through our hands—
A tangled dance that no one understands.

Each day's a puzzle, missing half its clues,
Yet still we march, though bound to win or lose.
Our shoes grow thin, our feet may start to ache,
But in the chaos, joy begins to wake.

Like starlings shifting, swirling through the air,
We drift, we soar, connected everywhere.
The trees extend their roots, reach toward the sky,
Their fruits a gift, while seasons pass us by.

We curse the clock, the tasks we cannot tame,
Yet laugh, for we all play this clumsy game.
And when we stumble, still, we rise again,
United by the humor in our pain.

For every path, no matter how undone,
Reminds us in the end—we are all one.

The Mad Dance of Hooves and Dreams

My first-born kin, two reckless twins,
Were raised where dust and madness spins.

One took bulls, the other broncs,
They lived for cheers and cowboy honks.

"The saddle's home," their father swore,
"Learn to ride, or kiss the floor."

One kicked high and soared in flight,
The other clung for eight—half-right.

A rib cracked here, a boot flew there,
Yet both still grinned, as if to dare.

One twin fell, and time stood still,
The other rode with half his will.

The saddle waits, the dust turns cold,
The tales of twins are softly told.

Yet somewhere past the rolling plains,
Their laughter rides through endless reigns.

In memory of Clinton and Clayton—world champion
bull and bronc riders.
Your courage still rides in the wind.

Inventor of the Void

He built his life with spark and steel,
A wife, two kids, the full ideal.
His house sang low with silver tones,
His name etched deep in civic stone.

Yet often stared he toward the skies,
A hunger burning in his eyes.
"There must be more," he softly said—
Then vanished into stars ahead.

Through wormholes bent by time and thread,
He found a world where none felt dread.
The trees were blue, the air was kind,
The people shared a single mind.

No grief, no joy, no death, no birth—
Perfection smoothed the edge of earth.
All spoke the same, all thought as one—
No passion stirred, no deed undone.

He lived among them, day by day,
But something vital drained away.
He missed the clash, the flawed delight—
The heart that breaks to birth the light.

So back he flew, through cosmic seam,
To find again what makes us dream.
He kissed the soil, embraced the known—
There's no place like a world full-grown.

And stars still call... but not today.

A Texas Sonnet

The golden cage of the sonnet
for early poets
    with lives in confined spaces
    along narrow streets
    shadowed by high brick facades
influenced the contrived form
of locked rhymes in fourteen lines.

The cage no longer golden
for a Texas poet
    who lives in an open terrain
    where soft grasses move with the wind
    and bonnets of blue waltz across the land
giving the poetic spirit freedom to design
seamless verses that flow into their own frame.

Unlikely Encounter between a Him and a Her

Through oversized dark glasses, she spied
the pristine, metallic sublime green Chevy
atop spinning extra wide, bold wheels
reflecting the noonday sun.

Her usual speed for safe traveling,
always one notch below the limit,
was replaced with a need to gaze
at the exotic coupe
moving with sheen and speed
from one lane to another
and then to another.

The silver grays, she and her Focus,
gained on their moving pursuit,
front bumpers and windows aligned,
with the feminist grandma
honking at the carefree young man
driving his sun-blessed car while
jamming to blaring Latin rap.

Feminist? Machismo? Age? No matter
for she just had to holler, "Love the car!"
The rapping driver side-glanced her way,
then quickly looked again in disbelief
to hear her yell one more time,
"Love the car!" Hearing her truth,
he grinned like a star on wheels.

He drove west, as all Huck Finns do,
she headed south, like a good snowbird,
appreciating his back window sticker
            —Tejas man—

Alkaline and Gall

Who is this creature
Born of alkaline and gall?
Who is it that regrets
The trip down the birth canal,
Cracking skull plates
Until the dark gates
Open to seawater?

Where can we find
The last lost son
In his final moments?
He is whispering through diseased teeth
Covered with salt and wax
About tides and sins
Kept in tins
At the back of the cortex.

The cinnamon bite of the sunlight has gone
Ground up by the molars.
Where is June's little boy?
He is among the clover 57 years ago
Under a clothesline
Giggling at the glow of translucent sheets
pinned to nylon
Blown by a wind that smells of pollen.

Slow Motion Lightning

I have been alone
A stone's throw from conviviality
A bone break from reality
Sucked in, spit out
To be coughed up on beach
In a baptismal rain.

But you..glow with slow motion lightning
In your eyes.
Your fine stitched nightmare
Strapped in long barrel rage
Across your back
And the hate mask blinding your eyes.

We…were torn on tusks of the black dog
That crawls hairless under the rug
Stirring a storm of needles.

In our kingdom, which is up for sale
A few pixels popped our eyes out.
Is your face so pale
Because of the store bought doubt?
Is it the purpose you can't live without?
We should be the kind of people
They don't know how to write about.

Putting the Moon to Bed

Clouds clash to see
who gets to pull a blanket
over the moon
in her bed.
Cozy in her misty wrap
she smiles.

In the dry times
when every spring fed
body of water is limp
lying tired, that's when
the moment comes to bite off
the chunks of time given you.

The moon turns her face on us
and the unbearable is born
the uncatchable is caught and we are awake
to re-awakening the glowing spots
of eternity caught in a temporal web
burning themselves out
to become the forever changing
always was always will be.

I see you now
bent in to a mountain shape
backlit, untouchable in our bedroom
attracting a soft blue
light to your contours.
my own bedded moon.

Love Song to the Dark

Aquifer- life sustaining water lives in the dark.
Lava roils in the belly of the molten deep
Diamond, emeralds, sapphires, amethyst
Ocean creatures, the Abyss, mermaids, tales
Chants, mystic ceremonies, incense, all
Thrive in the dark.

Seeds of life germinate in the dark.
Pregnancies are formed in the deep interior of joining
Owls, night birds, forests and stark mountain tops
Dwell in the dark.

We sleep, revive, and grow, and heal in the dark.
Stars, sprinkled throughout space, sparkle and shine
against the velvet black night.
The mountain crater is wrapped in history and shadows
We drive down its curves by the rising moon light
Campfires leap and enchant, sparks pop, songs are sung,
Camaraderie encourages new friendships
Venus shines on the jet-black ocean like a beacon!

Devoured cities reveal unknown secrets, ancient mysteries
Loved ones are laid to eternal rest under the safe depths
of their earthen blanket
Lovers whisper promises and intimacies.

Comets streak across the blackened heavens
Cosmic prophesy portends
Dreams are born, visions noted, deep wisdom is imparted
The Music of the Spheres reverberates
The evening cloak of quiet wraps a lullaby of peace around us all
And the hush of heaven holds us, in the dark.

Swans

I saw a pair of swans last night
Graceful in tandem upon the lake
Apparitions appearing through misty rain,
Bearing themselves in regal state.

Great waterfowl of heritage high
Ancestral lines of majesty
Gliding serenely and silently by
Beaks caressing necks tenderly.

The noble companions touched my heart
Recalling to mind that spring is nigh-
And courtship's course that joyfully brings
The promise of cygnets, by and by.

The Petroglyphs

In Olowalu, Maui where I used to live part time
Are petroglyphs on sacred cliffs that sometimes I would climb.
A marine expanse fantastic these heights revealed to me
Just half a mile before me lay the sparkling, living sea.

I turned around and there I found those ancient pictures still
A thousand years and yet preserved, emblazoned on the hill

I took a snapshot, brought it home and showed it to my son
Beaming with lore and history my tale had just begun-

"This symbol here shows that's a man."
"No way," he did conclude
Interrupting, pointing out
"This here is a Mer–dude!"

"Look at his legs, he has no feet." He pointed at a fin
I leaned to look and had to say that I agreed with him.

A merman? Well, now that makes sense-
Beneath blue sea and sky...
Reside a host of ocean folk
Well known in days gone by.

"It's plain that they're in Hawaii,"
I've heard locals insist-
"Not just in songs but now a days."
They swear the mer-folk do exist!

Lace Song

The explosion
        of my
                heart
when you died
stopped birds
        in mid-air
a forest of willow trees
                turned as black as widows' weeds
and clouds
        twisted into tight, thin threads

I lay
        very still
until my breath touched
        the wingtip of a lark
it's song like a bobbin
        weaving melody
creating lace from ash
        trees found their bright green
and my eyes
        noticed
the silver lining of the soft clouds

"...give sorrow words"

Let grief shine on the widow,
pierce the darkness of the word.
I add the letter "n" and create window,
which welcomes light and darkness
in equal measure, opens and closes
in all weathers. But lingering linguistics
confines and defines a cut out of a heart
and mind.

Let grief shine as fullness on the widow
'Widowe" to be empty.

Let grief shine as the wealth of life
"Vidh" to be destitute

Let grief shine as the precursor to joy
"Viduus" to be bereft

HOT CHOCOLATE

The brightness of the day is faded,
curtains shut tight against
winter's cold night, a welcome
quiet after rushing about,
a chance to imagine kingdoms
of cacao, feel the power
of jungles, tribes and rituals,
from the great Amazon River
to Ecuador, Mexico and Peru,
drink the magic potion
of the chocolate gods.
Taste the sweetness of new life.

Sonnet in Blue

Opaline silk weaves webs of refreshment
Atop the happily azure summer's pool
As sugary pup pops drip their portents
Guessing games and Rorschach blots that cool

Texas rainstorms rumble through cobalt skies,
Fuzzy lighting spikes soft air electric,
And sapphire sunsets backlight birds that fly
As what once was still becomes kinetic

What millions of dollars and countless jobs
Would a cerulean sweater uplift?
How crucial are the lapis seas that mob
The coasts, who birthed our life and fuel our thrift?

Ne'er has a shade meant more, I tell you true,
Than the sweetest bliss of your eyes so blue

This is our Jesus Year

Today we're as young as we'll ever be,
Our Youth is our penance, our purpose.
Try as we might, from time we'll never flee,
So, keep dreaming, screaming for purchase.

Today we're as old as we've ever been,
Grown up observing the world astonished.
With hindsight embracing our youthful sin,
Celebrating the edges we've tarnished.

And here's another solar return,
To teach us – and teach us again.
As incandescent within in us it burns,
Life itself is the meaning, my friend.

Oldest we've been and youngest we'll be,
Wise Witness of Wonder, cheers to thee.

There is no need to measure, all clocks have seized

Our senses now serve our combined situations and individual favor
For THIS is another world, no longer mired are we in shame & ignorance
The old world cannot perceive, nor divine this mysterious shift in fate
We are a kind of happy but not truly joyful born of actual suffering
Our bodies are finely tuned. Yet we cannot fully suppress our yearnings
Even increased intellect or by magnitudes via AI, we still ponder the stars
In this world it is all about brain power and outsmarting robots
Robots that don't sleep, have no guts or genitals, but take our jobs
Everything can be done for us as we command while we seek purpose
We share spaces and moments while seeking wisdom in computer chips
Holding each other is forbidden in some but required of others
This is a world of SILOS where you seek comfort with the like minded
Where does love fit into this world?
Where might love have a chance?
Where are flowers growing in our dystopian new world?
We were warned
Where is the world we knew and the one we once heard about?
Without labor and suffering, yearning, sweat, what shall fill our days?
The clocks are correct twice a day but are the hands are not moving

imagine friends melting time

imagine friends melting time, differing ages, TOGETHER A
SIMPLE poem WE rhyme

YES wise far beyond years, no apparent fears, ready with open ears,
most anytime

yearning for dialog, sharing ideas, observing, conveying, composing,
arranging

journals of life and images reflecting precious insights and special
moments
~IN TIME! ~

"time time time is on my side" sings Mick Jagger

"time of the season for living" sings Rod Agent

"one moment in time" sings Whitney Houston

SO MANY SING OF TIME AS TIME PASSES,
AS THEY PASS AS WELL, BUT NOT FORGOTTEN...

IMAGINE BECOMING A FRIEND WHO LASTS FOREVER
WHILE TIME ITSELF IS MELTING!

"YOU'VE GOT A FRIEND" SANG CAROLE KING

"YOU'VE GOT A FRIEND"

:::try it anyhow:::

I contemplated so much it made my head hurt
eyeballs dry and weary like used ballbearings
pages of books, studies, philosophy, history, and more
but it was always much simpler that all that really
nature gives us air to breathe, clouds and stars to ponder
like poems streaming in our thoughts brought forth from yonder
gaze upon the blue sky and the carpet green and sea foam sheen
and the way the light falls upon a lovely mermaid's skin
this is the art of seeing, imagining, so less taxing,
a yoga pose with eyes closed thinking of nothing at all
for the brain is like a busy hard-drive spinning endlessly
I say clear it clean! store away what needs keeping be
much room is needed for the mind to imagine and create
I contemplated so much it made my head hurt
but now I live for art first and what is given freely
it's not easy at first but worth it I say...
try it anyhow

AUSTIN POETRY SOCIETY

Playing Word Games

I sprinkle hints,
seeds in the withering garden
of your brain,
hope words will sprout,
blossom on your lips.
But deep in the gray matter,
atrophy spreads like a biblical pestilence.
In that un-Eden,
hummingbirds dart,
like crazed syllables,
scatter alphabets
like fallen petals
amid stems of thought—
bare, but pretending to be
bright. Colors for flowers,
all I could expect.

All you could expect:
bright—colors—flowers
bare, but pretending
amid stems. Thought
petals fall,
like scattered alphabets.
Syllables unleash darts
like crazed hummingbirds
in that un-Eden's spreading
biblical pestilence. Pushing up
through gray atrophy,
the blossom on your lips:
hope. Will words sprout
in your brain,
green the withering garden
if I sprinkle enough seeds?

The Crossing

I am going home on the early boat.
The pale, morning clouds muffle my passing.
The drowsy harbor hush-hushes the wake
to ripples and whisperings of parting.
Oh, I bought my ticket a good time back
when your mother went. She loved the ferry,
its comings and goings sure like the tide.
Bringing and taking away.
She is my beacon as the boat rounds the point.
I throw my penny—I am coming back
in sea diamonds and argyle waves at the rip,
but now the scalloping season is done.
With the sweet gift of knowing from her to me,
I give myself over to this crossing.

Listen

to my beehive clock, its tick of minutes, chime
and gong of hours, its pendulum loving
cajoler through my teens – the old timey
pull on my rush, the comfort of rubbed walnut,

surely crafted by a joyful man and sturdy
whose well-versed hands read the wood's grain,
who hummed as he sawed making his careful kerf
cuts, who smiled to remember honey's taste,

the harvest from hives woven of straw and wicker,
the same shape into which he eased veneers
to curve and meet at gentle point, this shelter
he sent to Seth Thomas, this hive for brass gears

and spiral springs I've wound for sixty years
to catch the muffled hum of abiding bees.

MOST POETS

Most poets don't appear
like Walt or Emily –
not wind-blown nor demure,
eccentric, wise, giddy,
charismatic, austere,
extraordinary.

Most poets look like us
at the grocery store.
Later, hidden, words rush
with insistent candor
finding form from the flux:
flesh and the trusted chore.

LITTLE RAVEN

Once upon a breakfast dreary
while my vision was quite bleary
and a baby raven stared at me –
it was daring, stolid, glaring,
wondering if I was sharing
any little tidbits it could see.

Indistinctly I was thinking
it was petulant, unblinking,
and I could not shoo this thief away.
It kept standing and demanding
with abysmal reprimanding
till I felt a dismal dark dismay.

"Take my donut, little creature,
may it satiate your feature,
let me sup my coffee now in peace.
Surely there are other victims
you can torment with your dictums
till you flutter utterly obese!"

Take a few moments
And gaze on the stars above.
Name one for yourself.
Keep this moment forever
And never tell anyone!

SWAMP FOR

Britain's Red Coats marched in waves.
Carolina's troops failed to save
American generals, Sumter and Gates;
Surrendered, the Charlestonians await,
Too outnumbered for open battle,
This daring general from his saddle
Commanded his Swamp Fox band
Through Pee Dee River to Snow Island.

Swords sculpted of saw blades
Butchered British in surprise raids;
Bullets from melted pewter plates,
Rescued prisoners for many states;
From farm boy to lieutenant,
This volunteer colonial militant
Remembering Cherokee strategies,
Led Red Coats to watery obsequies.

Swallowing scents, the crypt of bogs,
Devoured the dirge of Red Coats' dogs;
Baffled British yielded ground,
To the Swamp Fox band, victory found;
Freedoms lost were the strength of his few,
When the Swamp Fox marched, Britain knew;
Apparition of a foggy balm, the patriots call
Francis Marion, the shrewdest soldier of all.

TREES

I thought that I would never see
A poem lovely as a tree.
A tree that adorns an azure sky
And bends and bows as birds soar by.

A tree that covers heaven's streets
With leaves to warm celestial feet;
Upon my grave, I feel its roots
And I still in my poet's boots;

In time, beneath its verdant beauty,
I've had a rendezvous with duty,
A poem and God, a tree and me--
The difference was mortality.

LE JOUR DIEU PLEURA

Le jour Dieu pleura,
Le ciel pluet des balles,
Les edifices sont devenus sombres.
Les rues sont devenues les veines rouges de la cite geant,

Le jour Dieu pleura,
Je l'ai vu courir dans les rues,
  sans pistolet, sans artillerie,
Je l'ai vu se casher sous l'escalier,
Je l'ai vu porter les enfants blesse's.

Le jour Dieu pleura,
L'ignorance derangea la patrie;
L'inconnu a laisse' certains
  ignorants de
  l'importance de Humanite'.

Qu'est-ce q'un jour dans l'eternite?

Dans l'esprit de l'homme, c'est une vie en entier,
Quand le jour est en temps de guerre.

THE DAY GOD CRIED

The day God cried,
The sky rained bullets;
The streets became red veins of the giant city,
The buildings became sombre.

The day God cried,
I saw him running thru the streets,
    without a pistol, without artillery;
I saw him hiding under the stairs,
I saw him carrying wounded children.

The day God cried,
Ignorance disturbed the homeland;
The unknown left some ignorant
    of the importance
    of Humanity.
What is a day in eternity?

In the human mind, it is a lifetime,
When the day is in time of war.

Coconut Grove

A visit to the public clinic often means
a lecture and humiliation,
but not this time in the portable
building underneath the palm
trees, the diplomas in Spanish,
the old Cuban doctor tells
us that he likes "thin babies",
listening to her heartbeat,
looking her over carefully.
I think back to when we
waited outside the embassy
in a long line, the Honduran
mother expectant, pink
bougainvillea along white walls,
mango slices in a clear plastic
bag, inside an official
was condescending
to both of us, taxicabs waiting
outside, some from Brazil,
Russia, cars we forgot about
a long time ago. The yellow sun
above us, Elizabeth is happy
in Coconut Grove, talking
about people saying you are
a bad mother if you have a
"thin baby", I carry my daughter,
I can smell the ocean not too far away.

On Sunday

I think our lives end like a transformer
blowing up in white sparks. A hawk
sits on this one. Below is a red and
white pony already in the shade. On
Sunday is when we think about life
and death. A red truck is hauling oil
on this country road. A cornfield
stretches out near a brown river
flowing under a red rusted railroad
bridge. It is going to be a hot day.
We might also go up like a loblolly
pine tree in a brush fire lit by a match.
I read from a diary of a woman that
survived the pandemic 100 years ago.
She talked about taking walks on
Sunday and looking at the flowers.
She wrote about eating persimmons
when they were ripe. Little white
churches are waiting. Most people
are just thankful that they are still alive.

The Wig

Dignified, stately,
I was going to argue
that separation of
powers also meant
a division of labor,
specialization, but
it fell off, a horse
stepped on it, a man
spit tobacco on it,
it turned brown, a
cat was seen playing
with it and I decided
not to go, smell it
all day, deal with
the blue jay, Madison
and his jokes, or have
Franklin, the others
stare at it, whisper,
faction against me.

Breakfast At Marta's

Marta has prepared a breakfast this morning.
I sip the coffee and Marta peels a tangerine.
There is Marta in a photograph on the table,
    A ten year old smiling face;
And there is Marta peeling a tangerine
    And there is Marta nursing her baby
    And there is Marta watching her children play
    And there is Marta receiving their letters
    And there is Marta smiling through her wrinkles
    And there is Marta peeling a tangerine,
Sipping coffee,
And smiling at me.

The King in Yellow

The winds from Carcosa howl in pain,
Their blood drips down in tortured rain,
Searing hanging nerves of the human brain;
The King in Yellow has returned again!

Criminally insane his followers are;
They're behind the seat of your speeding car
To slice your eyes when you've gone just-so-far.
The King in Yellow is engaged in war!

His soldiers rule the government,
Surveil your home, collect your rent,
Then preach that *you're the one who must repent.*
Your room becomes their favorite lair,
Try to escape but no matter where,
The King in Yellow is waiting there.

Needs

I have no idea what the world needs,
but our grass needs
a break from the heat
my shoulders need
a massage
the dog needs
more enthusiastic fun
the TV needs
to spit out the winning numbers
from the goldenrod-and-orange blossom ticket
on the table, the typeset numbers standing
sturdy on the flimsy
page, waiting to preen themselves
when they are called
by She of the Hairspray and Silicone
on Channel 7 – her hand
in the cookie jar and my hand at my throat.

Colony

As the mysterious lady changes
shape and the werewolves cower
at the shifting, we trust
your telescope too much.
Can you see the colony
of people living on the rock? What
confidence to build
within the lunar light. What
ants we seem to them.

Watch them bounce
on the ashy inflexible--
gravity is a suggestion.

We forecast a *laissez-faire*
approach to oxygen helmets,
a daily celestial howling,
the measured breaths of a lonely billionaire.

Maybe the celestial snack bar is open
for the season at the Sea
of Tranquility.
Maybe they serve Moon Pies.

Farmer's Market

A Saturday morning, and I've already
bought a bushel of
chard that I
don't know how to cook.
Eggplants loll, fat on the
farmer's stand,
gorgeous eggs ready to blister in the
hot summer sun. Maybe
I shouldn't
jump to conclusions—maybe I won't
kill these plants before I
leave this parking lot. I smell the
mushroom booth ahead and the
Napa cabbage crates beyond.
Oh, how desperately I want to
pluck every tomato,
quietly hold it to the sunshine and
revel in the red.
So, what if I have a black
thumb? The market is bustling with
underachieving gardeners. I buy more
violet seeds for my
wayward garden, mostly to see the color
explode in the springtime. A
youthful volunteer offers me some
zinnias. Bags full of hope, I start for the car.

In the Beginning: An Egg, a Mask, a Woman

Oval, tap, tap on the counter.
Tap it, not too hard, but firm.
Pop, sizzle, congeal into white.
Satisfy our hunger, Mother.

The white, oval face of the oldest Goddess,
Bird Woman.
Her beak, the crease down the center of Her mask.
The Greeks wanted us to remember this,
showed us at the beginning of their Olympics.
The One who was older than Athena,
more ensconced in nature than Artemis.
Bird Woman flew across the stage.

But She was once small and voluptuous,
rare and precious
like you, young woman.
Back then, everyone honored you,
held you in the palm of their hands.
Men, women, boys, and girls
praying for nourishment,
for protection. All of us, trusting in you,
in a woman who looks just like you.
Your hips, breasts, and thighs; and mine,
before our bodies sold everything to everyone.
When women were the original carvers of women.
When they, She, and I
made this pocket-sized goddess
and placed it in your hands.

The Missing Norwegian

He left home mid-winter morning, humming,
"In the beginning, there was fire and ice.
Flick a little fire on the ice.
Slip a little ice on the fire.
Fog it is, and fog is mist."

He awoke next day, caught a fever,
shook with chills
stranded by a change in weather
a hole in his boot,
toes so cold, they burned.

One man in ninety
fishing the fjords
alone in the cliffs
hidden by mist,
the odds are…

He savors his aura
as his soul retreats
to the crevices of his cheeks,
listening from his skull
to fear and sweat, blood and breath.

Known as a quiet man
who plays the frame drum,
his gently ways falter
as his skin blackens
and his muscles twitch.

He bargains with the Fates, "If I live…"
He measures his remaining strength, his rope,
the odd point of his knife.
He knows he must make mist
from the powers of fire and ice.

AUSTIN POETRY SOCIETY

Of the Blues and You

In the shadow of a rock,
I cling to your mountain,
walking sideways uphill.
The blues rush like waterfalls
from my fingertips as the piano sings
in this new language,
because I never could play the blues
before this trouble.
You said, "That's how it goes."
Now, I know the deep patient
waiting to drop the notes just so.
How a tumble of notes can wail high
and moan low
and still drop the chord on time.
Just so someone else can know
the soul can communicate this:
To lay back in the cut.
To wait with energy,
tugging hard on gravity.
To walk sideways
up a mountain, in a spiral
around the solid rock of you.

Black Bird

It's 10 pm, time for hot shower
my nightclothes in hands
i move to the bathroom
suddenly, i convert into a black bird
flying heavily in the room
my left wing tilts towards the floor

stop it, stop it, i shout loudly
no sound comes out
the bird throws me on the floor
hitting hard to the wooden frame
of the bed and disappears

i am sitting in a whirlpool of dizzying pain
struggling hard to catch my breath
I hit phone number with knuckles for my son

i try to knit words out of deep pain
he quickly lifts me from the floor
places tenderly on the bed
flames of burning pain whip through my body

in the emergency clinic three x- rays
showing my right fractured shoulder
perfuse inner bleeding purpling my right arm
nurse tightly wraps my arm to the chest in a sling

in shoulder surgeon's clinic
dr. Zinger questioned if I fell forward, sideward or backward
'dr, i changes into a black bird
which threw me hitting hard to the bed frame'
his eyes widened in disbelief
looking deep into my eyes
he mumbles a bird, a big black bird?

" I will repeat the question again and asked…
my eyes swim in tears

AUSTIN POETRY SOCIETY

Woe

pain is merciless
slow moves its lava
in the dark veins of mind

a hard lump sticks
at the back of throat
neither it slides nor
it comes up

suddenly, a strange
sound erupts of
a hunted animal
in the larynx

like a smoke it rises
from the belly
where salt hills
have mushroomed up

now rotten and melted
all punctured
a tsunami of tears
smudges all over the face
cleansing the deluge

Agony

breath rattles like pine cones in the throat
i stumble into the shadows of fear
brush against a shroud of doubt

my eyes fix on rain blotched windows
and the road beyond where ghosts
of vehicles slice through the fog

in the distance the noise of ambulance
call to me: Shubh…Shubh…Shuub
it's echo dies in the stale air of the room

i wait for the sound of his footsteps
beyond the closed door
for rasp of his key in the lock

Little Ugly

If at the end,
your eyes are like veils,

may they draw on me.

If your face is a shroud,
may it hide my own

at the end.

But if you wake,
I will tell you, friend,

I love you NOW—
not just for who you

could have been
in the sun.

Swoon

Under the first front,
at last,

I wake to find your poem,
airy and intact.

Intact, meaning, it is whole.
It is nearly a person, the way it breathes.

Good morning! Good morning!
So cold. So clean.

Sally

Fiddle-dee-dee-faced, you were my first, Sally.
The mouse-brown braids, and wee, ironed-on mouth
must have fallen off by now.

I imagine those felt lips, old as mothballs,
awaiting some disembodied head, a bit of glue,
a thumb prick, stitch or two.

I took a ride in a mirrored elevator today, Sally.
My hair is perfect, but my mouth?—a lost element,
with no real say in this office place.

"You're such a doll," Greg says. *Greg!*

We've got to find our mouths again, Sally. We've got to!
We've got to stick together, me and you.

The Flow

The Flow

Have you felt the flow?
That fabulous field of forgetting oneself
And falling face first into the fullness of being?
I wish I could stay there, wish I could live my life
Where my painter's hand and eye form a straight line
Between my heart and this world of things
There are times, like now, where it seems so possible
To tiptoe to that water's edge and collapse into its current
To feel the crisp connection of surface on skin
And then the rolling weight of underwater winds and streams
Spinning and scratching along the stony, silty bed
Broken and healed in one fell motion
Hair and shorts filling with just the right mix
Of effortless connection and grit
And then, perhaps, it would be possible
To breathe in that strange air and sink
To become part of the roll itself
No more than a motion, an arc
A brushstroke
The expression, the thing itself and it's making

Regret

You know her, don't you?
Regret? The daughter of Hope and Loss
She was born in May, I think, of good intentions
or maybe it was August, of none at all
She was always living in her sister Disappointment's shadow
And cast her own long shadow
On that younger sibling, what was his name?
Oh, right, Possibility. Whatever happened to him?
She had a habit of overstaying her welcome
And even when gone
Was always moving back in with one relative or another
Forgiveness kicked her out twice
Though Exhaustion always left a key under the mat
Now grown, with children of her own
She still finds herself alone
Only Anger, her eldest, visits on holidays
While Wisdom has been estranged since he could drive
I try not to make too close acquaintance with her
But am friendly on occasion
As old friends who've outgrown each other tend to be
Besides, she tells great stories

Moses

Moses wore a veil
When he came down the mountain
So the people
Who couldn't see
Wouldn't see
That he saw what he saw
His skin shining so deep
In its melanin that the
Divine could not be doubted
That the seeing couldn't be unseen
The singing unsung
And once sung, the ear
Could no longer ignore the call
The eye, the light
The tongue, the transformed mind
My brother, take off your veil
The season to shield has set

I Can't Play With You Anymore

It's been a real blast hanging out
Swapping stories fanciful and true
But I've done all I possibly can
To lighten many loads
Forces greater than myself have announced
That I can't play with you anymore
Hopefully we'll meet up again
Laughing at how our residence down here
Was a mere opening act
In preparation for the amazing show ahead
You needn't be overly sad
I've got faith that the tragedy isn't forever
We're meant for something special
Fear comes from not knowing exactly what
And not being allowed to come back to explain
Don't bother with guarded optimism
How can bright light penetrate
If your blinders are too tightly bound?
Transition starts now
I'm convinced that we'll play later

Lucky Penny

Not long ago I found a lucky penny on my street
Thought I'd better put it in my pocket
Lest a chance at good fortune pass me by
And so the deed was done
Knowing errands needed doing that I took off at once
With that lucky penny held close to the vest
I imagined how I could do no wrong
Boy was I ever mistaken on that score
I forgot to get a loaf of bread from the supermarket
Tripped over a crack in the sidewalk
Resulting in an unplanned knee bruise
As I rounded the corner heading for home
Some hoodlums put the fear of God in me
When they rolled down the window of their cheap car
And called out disparaging names
Laughing as they sped off
Looking down once again at my pocket
I realized the penny didn't symbolize fortune alone
In certain cases luck entails what doesn't happen
No bones broken
No automobile tragedy
At the front door I admitted
Where it mattered my good luck held hard and fast

.

Meat Suit

I'm here before you in naked glory,
Total disclosure for all to consider.
What's there to hide anymore?
Greater prospects under the hood perhaps.
Outside I'm merely a meat suit:
Good blood in,
Toxic air out;
Biology's eternal dance.
And I'm but a lone atom sidestepping loneliness,
Just parts and labor with their botched warranty.
We're checked out in junky jalopies,
Slaves to a gas cap that's prone to falling off.
No use in carping.
One day I'll peel it off completely.
Freed from pain and disappointment,
I'll be an angel's angel,
No longer Time's hostage.
Beauty everywhere I look.
An eternity's worth of space to amaze me.
Stripped of the mechanics, I'm my true self again.

Sunday afternoon

"the sky's the limit, george"
"the sky's the beginning"
Something, somewhere
is dying.
I watch the turkey vulture turn and wheel
across the empty frame –
a blemish
on an elsewise pristine canvas
—I am the frame, and the sky
's not blue, until you're told.

Drawing #4

there is light buried
in the light
of the streetlights' reflection
yes there is still more buried
you are
light
poured into a bottle
you are
never far
when I hush
I hear a sucking sound
from the pavement cracks
a song
so old

A conversation with a dead Swede while half-awake in my bed

Do you believe in God?
Then tell me what is this earth. What is this half-finished heaven?
I cannot. (I tear words out of the air with my teeth, and spit them
    on the floor.)
This half-finished heaven lies, dusty on the shelf
in the company of the skulls of unicorns
Just hold it to your ear, you will find
The warm air is freed, and rises.
He gives a nod.
I smell burning.

What is love? It is the open window.
what is the open window? the open window
is at the end of a long,
long corridor.
The wind: a permanent caress.
I have trouble drawing a breath. He speaks in sympathetic tones,
we live on rock pounded to sand. Yet you are wrong again.
Stand between two mirrors facing each other.

What is life? life is a frozen scene
It is in the space between-
shut up. tysta ner. focus. All poets must answer this before birth.
what is life?
A brief pause in an organ recital...
A string of expletives, rising to the rafters
the smell of bowels and burnt offerings.
the taste of spit, the taste of sweat, the taste of tears
a sinking object that sinks and sinks
scream, suck, sink—
It echoes, then the music resumes.

In Saint-Véran

each time I am two steps out my door I pause
to savor the stark colors of winter at altitude

I love the way it's been here for millennia and will be
for millennia more

here in Saint-Véran we are used to the cold
it is below freezing and snows
a few more inches every few days
snowshoes and skis are a way of life

by the fireside in the evening I think about
the blessings I enjoy here in the High Alps
I cannot describe the beauty
in mere words en anglais ou en français

I regret that I cannot share this with my wife
she passed three years ago shortly after we moved here
she had fever then a cough then she couldn't breathe
we went to the hospital in Briançon
they put her on a ventilator and she couldn't talk

I don't think she ever knew she was dying
I held her hand and spoke almost continually
I told her everything I could remember
about our life together and how much
I love her and always will—
I think she heard me until toward the end
then she was gone

here in Saint-Véran we are used to the cold

Galaxies

I step from forest to field
Without moonlight it should be dark
But the field glows as if covered
mid-summer by newly formed frost

Above me is a river of brilliance
Countless suns burning
In a broad band that stretches
From horizon to horizon

My breath catches I am so small
Beneath this infinite array
The vast silence overcomes thought.
My soul feels overwhelmed

Now I find myself lying
In the soft bed of the field
Constellations hidden in the sky
I sense myself vanish into awe

I am astonished by the magic
That must be left by angels
In this starlit sanctuary
There is no other explanation

I hear the hymn rising
From the galaxies above me
My soul joins in and will sing
Long after I leave this place

I Long to Leave

Back a hundred feet into dunes
Among tufts of beach grasses
There is a stone the color of sand
Undisturbed by mice or plovers

A name perhaps once there
No one searching for it
Mist off the sea the only tears
Buried dust of a deserted soul

There is no embrace but the wind
No warmth but the sun that will set
Another hurricane season coming
I long to leave this place

THE ARTIFACT AND THE ART

Holding a pad, a pen, a thought,
What leads us to this place
Overgrown with grape hyacinth?
If thought is a stream
How many trees must fall
To make a raft
To float these words
Out of time's oblivion
So we may breath them
In the dusty musk of a book?

The pen is without memory,
The computer an illusion.
Thought evaporates
Like summer rain
Yet now the scent of hyacinths
Is singed into your breath
With black ink and residue of tree
That turns blue, turns green,
A reborn spring meant to be
Forgotten like all others
Turned to artifact through art.

STOP TIME

We stretch the song
to an arrow
of northbound geese.
Long weekends
become a limbo
of lake and laughter.

We hold the kiss
till breath comes short;
sink in a lock
of love only
exhaustion opens.

We take the train
to Vienna, to Paris.
Rails loop over
in mobius memory.

Beauty freezes.
Time is an insect
locked in amber.

DAYS PAST

I

Sunshine steps
through remembered windows
picking its way past a dance
of dust motes.

A child's smile frozen in photographs,
plump laughter in black and white...

II

Carriage wheels bounce
over sidewalk cracks.
Streetcars clack past bronzed memories
of fruit stands and shops
with Hebrew letters,
everywhere a babble of Yiddish.

Elms fountain green
on pebbled paths in parks
with warm stone walls.
Brightness spreads
in new-minted eyes,
butterscotch thick on pavements.

III

Wrinkled hands stroke baby hair,
crooning, crooning,
an old song from a lost world.

Two Darks

There are two darks. I rest between them.
Grey Brother walks into the light.
Sometimes I walk with him.
There is the dark of the chapel
and the dark of the tomb. I know
I choose the former and the latter
will in time choose me. Every night,
I sit in the space between,
stretch to embrace both
without their lingering scent
clinging.

Burden

On a bench in the dying park,
sits a man with a story. It's heavy.
He tells it to anyone
who comes within earshot,
even pigeons. At first
he brought bread. They came
and he told them the story.
They don't come much any more.
He no longer brings bread.

After a person heard the story,
you could see the man brighten a bit.
After a bird, less so. The air,
hardly at all. At this rate,
it will take a long time
to tell the story down
to something he can carry.

Huff

I am sitting at Huff's table.
His plaque is faded by the sun.
Would he be disappointed
his table is now No Smoking?
Would it make a difference?
The barista who smokes doesn't
enforce the city's ban. Would
Huff move to a smoking table?
The smoking tables have
neither eves nor cover.
He was here rain or shine.

I often saw him here.
The convenience store
across the street
still displays his ode.
I wrote poetry in those days,
but wasn't serious. Poets
are the oddballs you pass
outside bars and coffee houses.
I've never met one in an office,
though they may seek shelter there.

Falling Asleep

My nose crinkles

and lips curve north,

my hands at rest

beneath my head,

the scent of your hair

staining my fingers

Blocked

There's dust on my shoelaces
mites atop the bookbag
I take to the coffee shop
when I decide I can write.

Stale crumbs crushed
in my cushion cracks
four water-turned-whiskey-glasses
guarding the ash tray of gray frustration
that drains and fills with each hour
tied to my desperate confidence

Torn ideas carpet the hardwood
worlds formed from crumpled up pages
and the merciless text cursor-
an intermittent wall taunting me
with emptiness
digital insult built of nothing but
the absence of poetry.

Calcium Cathedrals

When the world hadn't
any creatures
like us
this earthen gallery
a mere hollow
and wet fingers with artistic aims
inched
down
the newborn cracks

scooping out the limestone
by a fingernail-full.

A cup carved a day
karstic masons
erecting dance halls and chapels
calcium cathedrals
for the gods of unseen places
and the few who meet them

Air resting in unmixed layers
atop stone untrodden
but for my knees,
settled into the wet floor
listening to the
drip
drip
of creation.

Invasion of America

The People came in the time before,
spreading across the land
Living with the land,
sharing the land with the herds.
And the land was fertile and provided
for the People.
What was not needed was left by another.

Then, the Europeans invaded
Spanish, English, Portuguese and French.
From cultures that was taught to "own" the land
that harvested and stored the bounty of the land
that drew boundaries and built fences and walls
and what was not needed was kept.

And the invaders brought germs
and pushed the People off
Ancestral lands that provided plenty of
into "Reservations" that provided little.
Killed the herds of bison for fashion
and let the food rot. And then
took the land of the reservations away.

And now the People live in squalor
uncounted and unappreciated
as thy fight to exist, fight to honor
the past and all of our ancestors who
lived well with the land.
And the "civilized" invaders called the People "heathens."

Military Cemetery

The fallen have decayed long since
to enrich this foreign soil,
their marble monuments
now stand passively aloof
to speak of sacrifice and courage,
death, fear, and carnage.

Here, white on white,
the crosses flood the snowy slopes,
bearing three short lines
to chronicle each life, record each soul.
only these few words are left
to the relentless enemy.

Thousands of lives end here,
wasted by a war fought long ago.
For reasons we who've come to question
refuse to understand.

"This is where your grandfather lies, son
I never knew him either."

Last Soldier But One

Would I kill
so I could claim that it was
I who ended all war?

Or, would I die
were I the least soldier but one
so he would have no one left to kill?

Will-o'-the-wisp

Midnight in the garden
Where the will-o'-the-wisp
Lightens the path of the Souls
Leaving their graves
To assemble in joyful company
Remembering
Talking of a time
In a green land
Of happy and sad memories
Of kindness, love and betrayal
Beautiful stones
Or simple crosses
But in end…all the same
The garden turns dark
The will-o'-the-wisp are gone

Love Song

Let us meet at night
When the moon
Turns our bodies to silver
And our souls to music
We'll sing with the stars
And the night sky
Will whisper a love song

Solitude

Beyond the window
Into the garden
A climbing jasmine
On the fence
Silence, Solitude
The rose petals of sunset
Promise a night
Of peaceful slumber
A fox runs across the lawn

Upon this Shore

We rode here on the particle waves,
by the beach of life we fell
past, present, future all combined
in the timeless sea we dwell.

We came from over fields of dust
a nod from God we became thus
we yield to time and gravity
unseen force in this eternity.

The essence of our being stretched across the infinite realm
the cloth is rendered, soul is trimmed
God blinks, another entity cut
from the mortal fabric, a life form sprung.

Shade of skin, breadth of form
cast from where and when we're born
we breathe and shape a life from soil
and gather tribes to help our toil.

The breath you take is in my lungs
the song you sing is on my tongue
the steps you take are in my shoes
the pain you feel in me imbues.

We'll ride out on the particle waves
to a distant shore we'll turn
then drown in cosmic laughter
as the stars forever burn.

Of Horsemen and Boats
A psalm and tribute to war related PTSD

They rode with rough horsemen, they flew on iron boats
they showed the world mercy, they gave it scarce hope
they tortured their lives to save the bedamned
but little we pleaded could salvage the lambs
the ways of our warring are summoned from hell
we're wrapped in its jaws, we're rapt in its spell.

Release the horses, untether the boats
reach the bewildered and terrified hosts
make caring your east, kindness your west
from a world of indifference, endeavor to wrest
circumspection from north, transcendence from south
hold firm to the injured, unburden their doubts.

Now render them mercies, comfort their harms
salve up their wounds and bless their scorched arms
turn your back to the wailing of crowds and their lies
and embrace the care of the ones who have died
to the ways of the world and what men want from them
recall them as caretakers of life and scarred limb.

Falling

If I let go of life's moorings, will you catch me if I fall
        will you wrap your arms around me as I trip into the maw
        of the catchment of life's anguishes that find us by the day
        then soothe me with your sacred breath that quells the sullen night.
If you find me in a dreamy haze, with distance in my gaze
        take me to a hidden cove and swim with me in grace
        by the way that you hold onto me and swirl on through the fog
        if I drown in life's insanity, please save me when I fall.
If you see me in a ragged mess that life tries to inflict
        gather up the haggard lot of me you can't predict
        where we'll go... oh wait you know, our puzzle is now laid
        apply your wondrous gauze of care and hold me as a babe.

I'm falling

    Falling into love that captured our hearts

I'm falling

    I will hold you up when life pushes you down

You're falling

    Fall now with me but don't let me keep you down

We're falling

    In and out of step but return to our one.

Soothe me with your sacred breath that quells the sullen night
Soothe me with your sacred breath
Soothe me

Cathy Baumbach. "A Cliché of Months", First Place Winner, Austin Poetry Society Annual Contest "Light and Lyric", 2021.

Claire Vogel Camargo. "a whirlwind tour", first published *Last Train Home*, Ed Jacqueline Pearce, 2021. "on the night train" first published *Last Train Home*, Ed Jacqueline Pearce, 2021. "empty arid earth" first published *Last Train Home*, Ed Jacqueline Pearce, 2021.

Lorrie Castellano. "Retirement" published in the *Poetry at Round Top Anthology*, 2025.

Janelle Curlin-Taylor. "The Horned Toad" Austin Poetry Society Annual Contest Spoken Word tied for First Place, 2024. "HOLD FAST" published as "Hold Fast" #2 in *Texas Poetry Assignment #19 - On Edge* 2/24/22.

Sergio Elizondo-Góngora. "The Arizona Baptism" Austin Poetry Society Annual Contest Patrons Prize, 2022. "Optics Taught by Ms. Alice, 2008" published in *Chrysalis: Literary and Arts Journal*, Fall 2023. "The Next Stage, 2022" published in *Chrysalis: Literary and Arts Journal*, Fall 2023. Second Place "President's Award" Austin Poetry Society Annual Contest 2024.

Nancy Fierstien. "Modern Day Civilian's Basic Training" First Place for "President's Award" in the APS Annual Contest, 2021. "If Forced to Change Color" published in *Blue Hole Magazine*, ed Mike and Joyce Gullickson, Georgetown TX Poetry Festival, 2012. Nominated for a Pushcart Prize. "Could There Be Such A New Creation? Second Place winner "Earth" Austin Poetry Society Annual Contest, 2022.

Amy Greenspan. "Blessed by Limestone" published in *Texas Poetry Calendar 2021* (Jeanie Sanders, Ed.), Kallisto Gaia Press, 2020.

Joseph Herrng, "The Little Boy in Me" Second Place Austin Poetry Society Annual Contest "Spoken Word", November 2024.

Terry Hill. "The Comedy of Being Us: We Are All One" First Place – Austin Poetry Society Contest, September 2024. "The Mad Dance of Hooves and Dreams" First Place – *Austin Poetry Society Contest*, March 2025. "Inventor of the Void" Third Place – Austin Poetry Society Contest, May 2025.

AUSTIN POETRY SOCIETY

Ailana Larson, "Love Song to the Dark" Winner - "Spoken Word" Austin Poetry Society Annual Contest, 2018. "Animals in the Wild" First Place "Best Austin Poetry" Austin Poetry Society Annual Contest 2018. "The Petroglyphs" published *di-vêrsé-city: Their Voices Still Ring, Annual Anthology of the Austin International Poetry Festival*, Editors: Stephen "Pete" Sebert and Dr. Charles A. Stone, 2020.

Susan Martinello. "Playing Word Games" published in *J Amer Med Assoc*, 322(7), 2019. "The Crossing" published in *Equinox*, Vol. 6, 2024. "Listen" published in *Mueller Magazine*, April 2024.

g. e. martt. "MOST POETS" Austin Poetry Society "Art of Poetry" award in 2024. "LITTLE RAVEN" first appeared on Facebook in 2016.

Benjamin Nash. "Coconut Grove" appeared in *Saw Palm*. "On Sunday" appeared in *Poetry South*. "The Wig" appeared in *RHINO* and the book *Sun*.

Benjamin Pehr. "Breakfast At Marta's" Second Place *Austin Poetry Society Contest* 2010/11. "The King in Yellow" Third Place Austin Poetry Society Annual Contest, 2023.

Mary Jane Philpy-Dollins. "Farmer's Market" First Place winner in "The Hope Contest" in the Austin Poetry Society Annual Contest, 2023.

Susan Rogers. "In the Beginning: An Egg, a Mask, a Woman" first published in *The Enigmatist*, Ed. Mike and Joyce Gullickson, 2017. Second Place in The Spoken Word Poetry Award Austin Poetry Society Annual Contest 2017. Also published as the title poem for *In the Beginning: an Egg, a Mask, a Woman*, by Susan J. Rogers, 2018. "The Missing Norwegian" Third Place in the "Person of Interest Award" Austin Poetry Society Annual Contest, 2013. *In the Beginning: An Egg, a Mask, a Woman* by Susan J. Rogers, 2018. "Of the Blues and You" 3rd Place in the "Music in My Soul Award" Austin Poetry Society Annual Contest, 2017. First published in *di-vêrsé-city, The Annual Anthology of the Austin International Poetry Festival*, Ed. Dr. Charles A. Stone, 2018. Also published in *Landscapes of the Mind* by Susan J. Rogers, 2020.

Thomas Smith. "In Saint-Véran" published in *MacQueen's Quinterly* 30 (September 15), 2025. Second Place "President's Award" APS Annual Contest 2024.

Bradely R. Strahan. "THE ARTIFACT AND THE ART" First Place in APS annual "Presidents Award" contest, 2023. "STOP TIME" published in *The Art of Losing* by Brick house books, 2011.

Jeffrey Taylor. "Two Darks" *Voices de La Luna,* September 23, 2021. "Burden" *Best Austin Poetry 2017-2018*. "Huff" *Best Austin Poetry 2018-2019*.

Jesse Taylor. "Falling Asleep" Second Place APS Aloha Award 2024.

Preston Tyree. "Invasion of America" published in *Wars Kill People*, 2024. "Military Cemetery" published in *Wars Kill People*, 2024. "Last Soldier but One" published in *Wars Kill People*, 2024.

Michael Alkus's poetic offerings follow a creative writing career that includes the syndicated newspaper column You Can't Make It Up!; creation of cable TV's Television Games Network; head writer and editor of the blogging service RealtyPLR.com; and book publishing with Inde Book Award-winning *Hit Woman* by Susan Hamilton. A former Chairman of the nation's oldest humor magazine, *The Yale Record,* he is also the post-graduate winner of Yale's Mayer Prize for Satiric Writing.

Cathy Baumbach was raised in the Midwest, educated at the University of Wisconsin (BA), and due to circumstance, now resides in Southeast Texas. Always a writer, she has rediscovered the thread that William Stafford said to 'never let go of.' That thread for Cathy is poetry. It bears witness to the sense of things: meteor showers; tangled fishing line; hummingbirds that fly over open water; breath; the lightness of childhood; the overall awesomeness of life—that sort of thing. Her work is published in *Touchstone,* the *Peninsula Pulse, Texas Poetry Calendar,* and *Visions International,* among others, as well as in professional museum publications and journals.

Joyce Benvenuto has been involved with poetry a long time. In fact, all of the periodicals she has appeared in are now folded—except maybe *Nimrod* that still hangs in there. Plus, all of their editors are now dead, so that closes that book too. Benvenuto has published four books of poetry since she retired at age 65. When working, she taught Creative Writing as a high school teacher for 18 years. She also created the Capital Area Poetry Contest for high school students in Lansing, Michigan. That contest awarded prizes for over 20 years. She has judged poetry contests for the Lansing Poetry Club and the National Society of Arts and Letters. She belongs to more than one writing workshop in both Vermont and Michigan. She has done public readings in person and on Zoom in Arizona, Vermont, and Michigan. She resides in both Vermont and Arizona. Benvenuto has three children and four grandchildren.

Birdman313 has been writing for most of his life. Originally from Benton Harbor, Michigan and a graduate of John Wesley College with a B.A. in Social Science, he also has an AA in networking admin from ITT-Tech and a computer tech certificate from JTI. Birdman313 has 13 published poetry books and 4 published poetry chapbooks, he has been published in several journals and newspapers. Birdman313 has several Editor's Choice Awards and one International award for his poetry. He has been a feature and guest on several blog talk shows along with open mic readings. He was presented a plaque for the poem "She", along with a gold medallion, and a pendant. His video "Forgotten Time" won first place in *The Light Poetic Ministry Poetry Video Contest*, his poem and video *Poems/Videos* featured on *Coffee Wine & Words* on Spotify and Apple Podcasts, Google, Anchor, *Reading Between the Wines*, *Journal of Expressive Writing* Authors Panel, *Lions and Pirates* Artist of the Month of June 2024.

Danielle Brooke is a poet from San Diego, currently based in Austin, Texas, where she works in health care policy. Her writing explores themes of grief, resilience, injustice, and personal transformation.

Charles Cann is a Retired Woodworker, Visual Artist, and Poet. Bachelor of Arts Degree in Sculpture from Rhode Island School of Design. Museum Curator at Plimoth Plantation a re-creation of the original Pilgrim colony in Plymouth, MA. Several years of Archaeology experience. 10 years of fine woodworking at his Cann's Works studio in New Bedford, MA. Creating one design furniture, wood carving, signs and Book Illustration. Been coming to Austin since 1970. Moved permanently to Wildflower Terrace in Muller in 2022.

Claire Vogel Camargo, a late bloomer, started writing on tissue boxes in the car and café napkins. Her free verse and Japanese short form poetry (her main focus of writing now) have been published in a number of journals, anthologies, and her book: *Iris Opening, an ekphrastic collection (2017)*. Her poems have placed or received honorable mentions in various contests. A past APS secretary, she lives with her husband in Austin, Texas.

Lorrie Castellano is a memoirist, poet, and retired clinical psychotherapist. A transplant from the Bay Area, her move to Texas as well as the quiet and isolation enforced by COVID gave her the freedom and time to reflect on life through poetry. As Margaret Renkl says: "The search for the right word to fill the right place can occupy a lifetime." *Still I Choose the Mountain,* self-published in 2023, is her first collection. Lorrie lives in Austin with her husband, Roger, surrounded by family, two majestic Live Oaks and the occasional visiting fox.

Janelle Curlin-Taylor is a Texas poet living in Tennessee. She inherited the poetry gene from her Texas grandfather and her mother. Published in various Texas journals and anthologies – including *The Senior Class: 100 Poets on Aging*, published by Lamar Press. Janelle is grateful to APS for keeping Texas and Texas poets close. She is married to California poet Jeffrey Taylor.

Sergio Elizondo-Góngora is a media professional living in Dallas. He has served as a commercial traffic specialist for many years, supporting KHOU-CBS (Houston), KENS-CBS (San Antonio), KVUE-ABC (Austin), WTHR-NBC (Indianapolis), KYTX-CBS (Tyler), KIDY-FOX (San Angelo), and WFAA-ABC (DFW). In 2022, he won the Patrons Prize from the Austin Poetry Society, and he has also been featured in college periodicals from El Paso.

Nancy Fierstien is a Dripping Springs poet who has spent 24 years sharing her works in anthologies and festivals throughout central Texas. In recent years she has gained acceptance of graphic arts submissions for publications too. Learn more about the poetry readings she hosts in her home and at the Dripping Springs Community Library by writing to nfierstien@gmail.com.

Amy L. Greenspan's poems appear in multiple editions of the *Texas Poetry Calendar* and in a variety of collections, including *The Senior Class: 100 Poets on Aging, Waco Wordfest Anthology 2023, Weaving the Terrain: 100-Word Southwestern Poems, Lifting the Sky: Southwestern Haiku and Haiga*, and *Haiku Presence*.

James M. Gregory. I do not claim to be a poet; I am a retired engineering professor. I write simple statements that rhyme more or less to tell a story. I have accumulated over 200 since my retirement in 2007.

Michelle Hartman is the author of four poetry books, four chapbooks, the most recent a winner of the John and Miriam Morris Memorial Chapbook Contest. Her work has appeared in *Crannog, Galway Review, The Atlanta Review, Penumbra, Poem, Southwestern American Review, Carve* and many more. She is the former editor of *Red River Review*, as well as the owner of Hungry Buzzard Press.

Joseph Herring joined the Austin Poetry Society in January 2024. He retired after owning a children's amusement park (Kiddie Acres) for 38 years. He was born in Beaumont, Texas but moved to Austin when he was one and has lived there all his life. He attended high school here and went to The University of Houston where he played football. One of his essays that he wrote in English class was printed in the literary magazine at UH. One of his teammates found out that he could write well, and he became the GO-To guy for prose and poetry. He is surprised that he did well writing because when he was in elementary school, it was a customary punishment for students who acted up in class to write on the blackboard 50-100 complete sentences how they would not repeat their transgressions. This form of atonement made him lose his zeal for English composition. Since retiring, he has found a new desire to write again despite his defiance to the early discipline he received. He doesn't know if he will ever be as accomplished at poetry as some of the members at APS, but should there be a need to write 50-100 repeating sentences, he is your scribe.

Terry Lee Hill was raised on the ranch lands and cotton fields of Texas and later served for over 40 years in public service in Washington, D.C., working in agriculture policy and training. Now back in Texas, he writes poetry rooted in resilience, nature, cowboy heritage, and spiritual reflection. His work has won multiple awards from the Austin Poetry Society and national competitions, with themes ranging from grief and healing to metaphysical exploration. Terry is the author of four published collections: *Whispers of Grace, The Eternal Whisper, Paths of Light and Shadow*, and *Aikido: The Path of Inner Balance*, all available on Amazon. His poetry invites readers to find strength, meaning, and comfort in the everyday trials and triumphs that define our shared human experience.

Irene Keller, Ph.D. In her past professional life as a Texas public school educator, she shared literature and poetry with thousands; present day, she writes poetry. Her poem "Unlikely Encounter between a Him and a Her," was published in *Assignment #68: Texas Cars*, June 2024, in the online journal, *Texas Poetry Assignment*, editor Laurence Musgrove.

Joshua Kight was born in 1954 in Virginia Beach, VA in to a working class home that fell apart when he was 9 years old. He spent a lot of time alone and learned to entertain himself through drawing and writing. Combining poetry with his paintings lead to writing poems that were stand-alone productions. He is married and has four children and one granddaughter.

Ailana Larson, songwriter, author, and award winning poet has toured the U.S. and Canada presenting her work on stage, through music, and publications. Co-founder of PlayFest, an Austin Children's Theater program, she created and performed her show *Bear Essentials- An Introduction to Sign Language through Story, Dance and Music.* Special Needs co-coordinator for 3 school districts, and teacher of the deaf and gifted she delights in the diversity of creative communication. Ailana's mission is to promote self-awareness and individual contribution through the visual and performing arts. She divides her time between Maui, Hawaii and Austin, Texas. Aloha!

Laraine Kentridge Lasdon attended the University of the Witwatersrand In South Africa. She also studied dance and taught little ones ballet in her aunt's studio. She studied drama, dance and music in London and pursued writing poetry. "It is the music of words that pulls me towards poetry as well as its magnetic storytelling opportunities." Laraine has served on the Board of Directors for the Institute of Poetic Medicine. Her husband was the late Leon Lasdon who supported and encouraged her to keep writing.

Bailey LeRoux is originally from Abilene, Texas, Bailey now lives in south Austin with her husband, Michael, and son, Rex. Bailey earned a Bachelor's degree in public relations & applied communication and a Master's in business administration from Hardin-Simmons University in 2014 and 2020 respectively. Professionally, she works on a wealth management team helping families plan for their financial futures and she is currently working to earn her CFP designation. When not in the office, Bailey enjoys yoga, crochet, live music, gluten-free baking and (of course) poetry.

Jack McCabe a.k.a. <@magicjackatx> Rhode Island born oldest of nine children. retired railroader, moved to Austin in 2011 after retiring from Amtrak in July of 2010. Creative: musician, songwriter, performer, poet, visual artist, photo and videographer Jack was born in Providence, RI, and named John Patrick McCabe, after his dad and two grandfathers. Educated in Catholic Schools by Sisters of Mercy order and in high school by Christian Brothers at La Salle Academy. He earned a BFA in visuals arts at University of Rhode Island as an adult student. He took on various jobs: Surgical Tech, Truck Driver, Toy maker, Shipping Agent, Delivery driver, Baggage clerk, Ticket Agent, Station Supervisor. He was a member of the Friends of Kingston Station board for a decade and inspired the restoration of the history

Kingston Rail station in RI. In Austin was President of TARA for a year. Pool committee lead at his OHA. Jack dedicates his music performing to elder homes and rehabs with various partner guests around Austin around 50 gigs a year. A member of the Austin Poetry Society for several years.

Susan Martinello lives in Austin, Texas. Her poems have appeared in *Birmingham Arts Journal, POEM,* the medical journal *CHEST, Connotation Press, 2nd & Church, Number One, The Museum of Americana, JAMA: Journal of the American Medical Association,* and *The Louisville Review,* as well as in *Whatever Remembers Us: An Anthology of Alabama Poetry, Panik Anthology,* and *Nancy Drew Anthology.* Her book *Little Gears of Time* was published May, 2020 by Negative Capability Press

Garrison Martt (g. e. martt) is a lifetime member of The Austin Poetry Society and has served 8 years as its president. He has won various poetry contests and also sponsored contests. His poetry has been published in several journals and chapbooks. He has also been a guest speaker for The Poetry Society of Texas, Poetry in the Arts and Expressions. Garrison founded *The Past Poetry Project* in 1995, a performance group celebrating the works of past poets. He has also been occasionally active in community theater for over 50 years.

Ruthan S. Meszaros (Houston, Texas)- B. A. Linguistics, English-Univ of Texas-Austin; Languages-ACC- *Who's Who Among Students in American Junior Colleges*; Lifetime Member Austin Poetry Society, served as Recording Secretary and Newsletter Editor Austin Poetry Society, poems published APS *50th Jubilee Anthology,* Member *Who's Who Austin Poetry Society.*

Benjamin Nash has *Sun* available at Finishing Line Press. He has had poems published in *Louisiana Literature, Tar River Poetry, 2River, Denver Quarterly, Southern Poetry Review, Pembroke Magazine,* and other publications. He has been a member of the Austin Poetry Society for 10 years. He didn't start writing poetry until he was about 40 years old. He enjoys reading, watching movies, and spending time with his daughter.

Benjamin Pehr is a member of the Austin Poetry Society and active in the Austin poetry community.

Mary Jane Philpy-Dollins, MSN, RN, MA, is a nurse, poet, knitter and a great conversationalist. She is a former President of the Austin Poetry Society and has previously published poetry in *Beginnings, medmic, The Poetry Machine: Volume 2, 2021, The Poetry Machine Volume 3, 2022,* and *The Poetry Machine: Volume 4, 2025* and in the *Waco WordFest Anthology 2023.* Her first book of poetry *Pulling At the Curtain,* was self-published in 2024. She lives in Driftwood, Texas with her husband and dog.

Susan J. Rogers has been interviewed about her poetry on the Texas Nafas program for Austin Public Access Station television. She has been a featured poet at Book Woman multiple times, including on the "Getting to Know the Goddess" series. Her poetry has been published in *The Ocotillo Review, Enchantment of the Ordinary* by Mutabilis Press, *di-vêrsé-city, The Annual Anthology of the Austin International Poetry Festival,* and *Blue Hole,* a magazine of the Georgetown Poetry Festival. Her books include *In the Beginning: an Egg, a Mask, a Woman, Landscapes of the Mind,* and *Sacred Grove.*

Shubh Schlesser has been published in T*exas Poetry Calendar, Di-Verse-City Anthology, The Borderlands Texas Poetry Review, Ardent Poetry in the Arts,* Austin Poetry Society, *Forest Fest Anthology Lamesa, The Enigmatist, Blue Hole, Galaxy of Verse, Austin Chronicles, San Antonio High Way, Big River Poetry Review* Baton Rough Louisiana, *Illya's Honey, Drash Pit, Muse India,* Taj Mahal India, *Verbal Arts India South Asian Anthology,* Frankfurt Austria. Her publications include the chapbook *Sacred River* poems from India, published by Sociosights Press, Austin, Texas April 2016 Poetry Book, *Small Small Joys* published by Atmosphere Press, USA, 23 January 2024.

Bronmin Shumway is a former Austin Poetry Society president (2013-2015). Now based in Chicago, IL, she focuses on her literary work, on co-songwriting with her husband, musician and teacher, Kirk Sonnenberg, and on being mother to daughter, Landon. Her first full-length collection of poems, *The Night You Were Born,* was released July 2025.

Jason Sierra is an artist and non-profit professional. He lives in the Austin area with his husband, their four children and a sheepadoodle named Kobe. He began his writing career as part of Stanford Church's Spoken Word Collective and adores the Episcopal Church's Book of

Common Prayer.

Greg Silver earned two college degrees with honors—an A.D. from Austin Community College and a B.A. from Concordia University—while actively participating in honors societies at both institutions. Following graduation, he completed an internship with the American Heart Association on behalf of the Texas Association of Mexican American Chambers of Commerce. Greg's professional career began as a Research Associate at Texas Energy Research Associates, where he processed corporate filings—a skill set that led to a 12-year tenure as an Administrative Assistant in the Office of the Texas Secretary of State. He continued working until symptoms of Young Onset Parkinson's Disease (YOPD) led to early retirement. A prolific, prize-winning poet since 1988, Greg's work has been recognized by the Austin Poetry Society. He is recognized by his friends as being a prize winner on "Name that Tune" games. His dream has always been to become a DJ. In 2012 he founded a music review blog which he named "Ear Buzz". A lifelong lover of books, he entered kindergarten reading at a seventh-grade level—thanks in part to PBS programs—and began volunteering as a library aide at an early age, including at Austin's main library. Most recently, he became a Yelp Elite for his restaurant reviews.

CE Smith writes from the threshold between dream and waking. His poems slip between ghosts, memory, and myth. He and his wife live in Austin, Texas, where they are building an experimental AI, a scent library, and possibly themselves.

Thomas Smith is a physician and former University Professor. He has written poetry for fun, family, and friends since high school. He spent 18 years on medical school faculties and has over 65 articles and book chapters in the scientific literature. COVID changed his creative focus. He began writing poetry seriously after his book in verse *The Search for King: A Fable* was published in 2022. His first published poem was in March 2023. He since has published over 130 Japanese short form poems (haiku, tanka, haibun, senryū, shahai, and others), free verse and rhymed poems, and limericks in a number of literary journals. He and his poems are listed in the *Living Haiku Anthology*. He lives in Austin, Texas, with his wife, three children, and four grandchildren.

Bradley R. Strahan taught poetry at Georgetown Univ. for 12 years. From 2002-2004 he was Fulbright Professor of Poetry &

American Culture in the Balkans. He has 7 books of poetry & over 800 poems published in *America, Texas Observer, Christian Century, Poet Lore*, etc., etc. & many anthologies. His poetry book, *This Art of Losing*, was highly praised as has his latest book of poems about his year in Ireland *A Parting Glass*. Both have been translated into French.

Jeffrey L. Taylor is a retired Software Engineer. Around 1990, poems started holding his sleep hostage. He has been published in T*he Perch, California Quarterly, Texas Poetry Calendar*, and *Texas Poetry Assignment.*

Jesse Taylor is a poet from Austin, TX and a member of the Austin Poetry Society since 2024.

Preston Tyree was born in Lynchburg, Virginia near the end of 1943. He has married twice and is the father of two children and six grandchildren. He has lived in many cities and visited over 25 countries. He started writing poetry in 1958 and is still writing. He has done a number of chapbooks including *Wars Kill People* and *Bicycle Poems* and one volume published in 1999 *Back Roads*. He is a long term member of the Austin Poetry Society.

Maria X. Wells, a Fulbright Scholar and Professor at the University of Texas, embraced poetry after retiring from academia. In 2010 she was invited to a meeting of poets and writers by a friend in Paris, where she wrote her first poem, "Memories in Silver". On her return, she joined the Austin Poetry Society to continue her interest in writing poetry. Her first book of poems *Images in the Clouds reading the sky* was published by Plain View Press, Austin, on February 14, 2022. It contains sixty poems and ten illustrations by the author. She has given readings at the Laura Bush Library, the UT Poetry Center, Book People, the Dell Jewish Cultural Center, and private book clubs. In the summer, she participates with her Paris friend in organizing a poetry reading on an island in Greece for poets of all nationalities.

Scott Whitehead. In 2017 he had an epiphany during a yoga class upon hearing the Rumi line "Speak little and learn the wisdom of eternity." He realized there was something brewing under the surface his whole life and the cover finally came off and he began writing. After prose failed to consistently convey what he felt, he discovered that he thinks in poetic cadences and herein lies the unfolding.

www.ingramcontent.com/pod-product-compliance
Lightning Source LLC
Chambersburg PA
CBHW051716090426
42738CB00010B/1938